SCHIRMER PERFORMANCE EDITIONS

TCHAIKOVSKY
ALBUM FOR THE YOUNG
Opus 39

Edited and Recorded by Alexandre Dossin

To access companion recorded performances online, visit:
www.halleonard.com/mylibrary

Enter Code
3646-0321-2778-7072

On the cover:
Couple on Horseback (1906)
by Wassily Kandinsky
(1866-1944)

ISBN 978-1-4234-8388-5

G. SCHIRMER, *Inc.*

DISTRIBUTED BY
HAL•LEONARD®
CORPORATION
7777 W. BLUEMOUND RD. P.O. BOX 13819 MILWAUKEE, WI 53213

www.schirmer.com
www.halleonard.com

CONTENTS

4 **HISTORICAL NOTES**

5 **PERFORMANCE NOTES**

12 Morning Prayer

Тихо [Calm] (♩ = 70-74)

13 Winter Morning

Скоро [Fast] (♩ = 84-88)

16 Mama

Умеренно [Moderate] (♩ = 88-92)

18 Hobbyhorse

Очень скоро [Very fast] (♩. = 110-120)

22 The Wooden Soldiers' March

Умеренно [Moderate] (♩ = 105-115)

24 The New Doll

Скоро [Fast] (♩. = 90-100)

26 The Doll's Illness

Умеренно [Moderate] (♩ = 60-64)

28 The Doll's Funeral

Медленно [Slow] (♩ = 58-62)

30 Waltz

Довольно скоро [Quite fast] (♩. = 62-66)

34 Polka

Умеренно (темп польки)
[Moderate (Polka tempo)] (♩ = 96-100)

36 Mazurka

Не очень скоро (темп мазурки)
[Not very fast (Mazurka tempo)] (♩. = 45-50)

39 Russian Song

Скоро [Fast] (♩ = 100-110)

The price of this publication includes access to companion recorded performances
online, for download or streaming, using the unique code found on the title page.
Visit **www.halleonard.com/mylibrary** and enter the access code.

40   Peasant Plays on the Accordion

Довольно медленно [Quite slow] (♩ = 60-65)

42   Kamarinskaya

Скоро [Fast] (♩ = 100-110)

44   Little Italian Song

Умеренно [Moderate] (♩. = 60-64)

46   Little Ancient French Song

Весьма умеренно [Very moderate] (♩ = 68-72)
с чувством [with feeling]

48   Little German Song

Очень умеренно [Very moderate] (♩ = 100-110)

50   Little Neapolitan Song

Тихо [Calm] (♩ = 80-84)
grazioso

54   Nanny's Tale

Умеренно [Moderate] (♩ = 100-110)

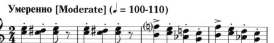

56   Baba-Yaga

Очень скоро [Very fast] (♩. = 130-140)

58   Sweet Dream

Умеренно [Moderate] (♩ = 66-70)
с большим чувством [with much feeling]

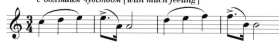

61   The Lark's Song

Умеренно [Moderate] (♩ = 110-120)

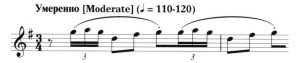

64   At Church

Умеренно [Moderate] (♩ = 58-62)

66   The Organ-Grinder Sings

Тихо [Calm] (♩ = 120-130)

68   ABOUT THE EDITOR

HISTORICAL NOTES

Pyotr Il'yich Tchaikovsky (1840–1893)

One of Russia's greatest composers, Pyotr Il'yich Tchaikovsky was born in Kamsko-Votkinksky, in 1840. A very sensitive child, he was attracted to poetry and music at a very early age; however, his musical education during his formative years was not very disciplined. After moving to St. Petersburg in 1850, Tchaikovsky was a student at the School of Jurisprudence from 1852–1859 and started working at the ministry of justice in 1860. His passion for music proved to be stronger, and he decided to make it his career. In 1859 the Russian Musical Society was created, and three years later, the St. Petersburg Conservatory offered its first classes. Tchaikovsky enrolled at the conservatory and soon after graduation in 1865 was invited by Nikolay Rubinstein (brother of Anton Rubinstein, the founder of St. Petersburg Conservatory) to be a professor in the newly created Moscow Conservatory, where he taught

from 1866 until 1878. Financially supported by patroness Nadezhda von Meck from 1877 until 1890, Tchaikovsky quit his conservatory position and was able to concentrate exclusively on his work as a composer. He died in 1893 of cholera.

Tchaikovsky is the composer of such masterpieces as *The Nutcracker* and *Swan Lake* ballets, the Piano Concerto in B-flat minor, the "Pathétique" Symphony and many other famous works. His passion for Russia is evident in all his works, many of which use folk themes; nevertheless, Tchaikovsky found a perfect balance between a Russian and Western European style, making his works accepted and admired both in Russia and internationally.

As a proof of Russia's admiration for his work, its most famed musical institution, the Moscow Conservatory, was renamed Tchaikovsky Conservatory in 1940 in honor of the composer's 100th birthday. Within its walls the first Tchaikovsky International Competition was held in 1958. This competition, whose first winner in the piano category was Van Cliburn, happens every four years and is unanimously considered one of the most distinguished musical events in the world.

PERFORMANCE NOTES

Introduction to Tchaikovsky's Piano Music

Tchaikovsky composed a great number of pieces for solo piano, most of which never entered the standard piano repertoire. The majority of his piano works are small pieces, often included in groups, such as Opp. 19, 21, and 51 (6 pieces each); *The Seasons*, Op. 37b and Op. 40 (12 pieces each); Op. 72 (18 pieces); and *Album for the Young*, Op. 39 (24 pieces).

Tchaikovsky's writing for piano is not always idiomatic, especially when compared with such pianists-composers as Rachmaninoff or Prokofiev. A prolific and expert orchestral composer, Tchaikovsky naturally gravitated toward orchestral textures when composing for piano. For this reason one should use a great deal of imagination to effectively "orchestrate" the pieces at the piano and convey an orchestral sound from the instrument. I strongly encourage anyone interested in performing *Album for the Young* and other solo pieces by Tchaikovsky to listen to the great composer's orchestral works, paying close attention to the way the instruments are used.

Album for the Young, Op. 39

In a February 1878 letter to his publisher Tchaikovsky mentioned his interest in creating a set of pieces dedicated to children. In May of the same year the composer finished twenty-four small pieces in only four days. The influence of Robert Schumann's *Kinderscenen*, composed 40 years earlier, is evident in letters and also in the original title:

Children's Album
Collection of Easy Pieces for Children
In the manner of Schumann

The collection of pieces was revised by Tchaikovsky in July of 1878. More changes were made in the set by the time it was published in October. The order of pieces was modified and some musical details differ from the manuscript. According to editor Thomas Kohlhase the reordering was probably done by the publisher for practical page-turning purposes. The order of pieces in subsequent editions of *Album for the Young* has been based mostly on this first edition. Despite the fact that this collection of pieces does not have a unifying theme or program, the editor agrees with Kohlhase regarding the importance of following Tchaikovsky's original order. This is especially true in the group of pieces 6–11 where Tchaikovsky seems to follow a story taken from the children's book *Les Malheurs de Sophie* by Sophie de Ségur. In this story children receive a new doll, break it, bury it, and have dances afterward. By changing the order for practical page turns, the literary connection is broken. In the altered order the "new doll" comes after the "doll's funeral," and the three dances are separated.[1] The present edition and the accompanying recording are based entirely on the order of the May 1878 manuscript, and are published in this form for the first time in the United States. While there is an edition of the manuscript published in Europe (Wiener Urtext Editions, 2000) and some Russian recordings that maintain the cycle in the autograph version, these are not well-known.

Fingering

Fingerings are editorial and have in mind a medium-sized hand. Some adjustments may be needed for smaller hands. In rare instances, the hand distribution has been changed, allowing smoother pedaling and/or articulation. All such changes are editorial since Tchaikovsky did not include any performance indications of this kind in his manuscript. As a rule fingerings were carefully chosen to convey the phrasing and articulation, not simply for comfort. Two numbers connected by a hyphen represent a slide between black and white keys; two numbers connected by a slur represent finger substitution. In some cases, an optional fingering is shown under or above in parentheses.

Pedaling

It is practically impossible to notate pedaling in an effective way. Good pedaling depends on so many variables (quality of the instrument, performer's touch, how far the pedal is depressed, specific acoustics, etc.) that any effort becomes almost pointless, since the performer will need to make the final decisions using his or her musical abilities and sensibilities. Therefore, pedaling is only indicated for a specific effect. In the sections where effective pedaling is almost impossible to notate or too obvious, it is omitted altogether. One should assume that the pedal needs to be used most of the time, especially overlapping pedal in legato chordal textures. Except for instances where a special sound effect is needed, good pedaling is not supposed to be heard. In other words, use the pedal so that the textures are always clear and not compromised by excessive blurring. The orchestral textures should be carefully practiced; the result should reflect the polyphonic richness of these works. In this Romantic music an indication of *no ped.* means to use as little pedal as possible (usually in very light, staccato textures).

Metronome markings

Metronome markings are editorial. Instead of suggesting a specific marking, a small range of possible tempos is provided. In the editor's opinion performances outside those recommended ranges may lack the necessary clarity if too fast, or may not allow for correct phrasing if too slow.

Dynamics and Articulation

Dynamics and articulation markings are Tchaikovsky's throughout.

Performance Notes on Individual Pieces

Morning Prayer

This piece would work very well in a choral setting. The four-part texture clearly implies choral singing, and the playing should reflect that. Syncopated (overlapping) pedal should always be used, and in conjunction with careful fingering, should bring out the best of this enchanting work.

Winter Morning

This belongs to the group of descriptive, nature-related pieces. The tempo marking "fast," together with the short, accented motives, create an atmosphere of cold Russian weather, when one is outside and needs to move quickly to get warm. Pay attention to Tchaikovsky's articulation and use a "down-up" gesture with your wrist in order to convey the accents.

Mama

The music is a very calm and relaxed description of the comfort that a mother brings to a child. The rocking accompaniment figure expresses the moment a child falls asleep in a mother's arms, while the right hand has a simple, repetitive melody typical of nursery songs.

Hobbyhorse

"Very fast" is the tempo marking for this exciting, playful miniature. It should be performed lightly, *staccatissimo* throughout. The loudest dynamic marking is *mf*, and a flexible wrist coupled with active fingers will be the recipe for success.

The Wooden Soldiers' March

Here is another playful work, this time a lovely march. Pay special attention to the composer's articulation markings, and use very little pedal throughout. The fingering indications should help you achieve the correct articulation and dynamics.

The New Doll

The first one of six pieces (6–11) probably related to the book *Les Malheurs de Sophie* by Sophie de Ségur (see introduction), this is a description of the happiness that a new toy brings to a child. Long melodic phrases are interjected with short motives, accompanied by a breathless figure. The texture and the choice of key remind us of "April" from *The Seasons*.

The Doll's Illness

Alas, the new doll is not new anymore… Too much excitement has made the doll "sick," and an ecstatic texture displays the sad mood that this illness has brought to the children.

The Doll's Funeral

The funeral procession is very solemn and the poor doll is put to rest. Tchaikovsky is very economic with the melodic line in this work, and one should observe the maximum dynamic marking of *mf*, keeping the overall dynamics at around *p* or *pp*.

Waltz

This waltz reminds in some ways of the final waltz from *The Seasons*. According to *Les Malheurs de Sophie*, after the doll's funeral, the children have merry dances?!—Tchaikovsky includes three dances in sequence after the three doll pieces. A great ballet composer, Tchaikovsky always feels comfortable with dance numbers. This waltz is not an exception. Follow the fingering indications for a nice and articulated performance.

References:

Scores

P. Tchaikovsky, *Album for the Young,* op. 39. Oxana Yablonskaya, ed. New York: International Music Company, 2006.

P. I. Tchaikovsky, *New Edition of the Complete Works. Series VI: Piano Works and Transcriptions.* Vol. 69b. Thomas Kohlhase, ed. Moscow, Mainz: Schott, 2001.

P. I. Tchaikovsky, *Kinderalbum, op. 39.* Thomas Kohlhase, ed. Vienna: Wiener Urtext Edition, Schott/Universal Edition, 2000.

P. Tchaikovsky, *Detsky Albom, op. 39.* Victor Merzhanov, ed. Moscow: Schott, 1992.

P. Tchaikovsky, *Album para a Juventude, op. 39.* Souza Lima, ed. São Paulo/Rio de Janeiro: Irmãos Vitale, 1957.

P. Tchaikovsky, *Album for the Young, op. 39.* Schirmer's Library of Musical Classics New York: Schirmer, 1904.

P. Tchaikovsky, *Album for the Young.* Miami: Kalmus Edition, Warner Bros. Publications, 2001.

Books

Piotr Ilyitch Tchaikovsky: Letters to his Family. An Autobiography. Galina von Meck, trans. New York: Cooper Square Press, 2000.

Audio Credits

Lance Miller, Recording Engineer
Alexandre Dossin, Producer and Pianist
Recorded at Beall Concert Hall,
University of Oregon School of Music and Dance

Comparative table between the autograph and previous published editions

Russian Title	English Translation	Key	Position in the Manuscript	Position in previous Published Editions
Утренняя молитва	Morning Prayer	G Major	1	1
Зимнее утро	Winter Morning	B minor	2	2
Мама	Mama	G Major	3	4
Игра в лошадки	Hobbyhorse	D Major	4	3
Марш деревянных солдатиков	The Wooden Soldiers' March	D Major	5	5
Новая кукла	The New Doll	B-flat Major	6	9
Болезнь куклы	The Doll's Illness	G minor	7	6
Похороны куклы	The Doll's Funeral	C minor	8	7
Вальс	Waltz	E-flat Major	9	8
Полька	Polka	B-flat Major	10	14
Мазурка	Mazurka	D minor	11	10
Русская песня	Russian Song	F Major	12	11
Мужик на гармонике играет	Peasant Plays on the Accordion	B-flat Major	13	12
Камаринская	Kamarinskaya	D Major	14	13
Итальянская песенка	Little Italian Song	D Major	15	15
Старинная французская песенка	Little Ancient French Song	G minor	16	16
Немецкая песенка	Little German Song	E-flat Major	17	17
Неаполитанская песенка	Little Neapolitan Song	E-flat Major	18	18
Нянина сказка	Nanny's Tale	C Major	19	19
Баба-Яга	Baba-Yaga	E minor	20	20
Сладкая грёза	Sweet Dream	C Major	21	21
Песня жаворонка	The Lark's Song	G Major	22	22
В церкви	At Church	E minor	23	24
Шарманщик поёт	The Organ-Grinder Sings	G Major	24	23

Посвящается Володе Давыдову

Детский альбом
Сборник лёгких пьесок для детей
(подражание Шуману)

Dedicated to Volodja Davydov

Album for the Young
Collection of easy pieces for children
(à la Schumann)

1. Утренняя молитва
[Morning Prayer]

Pyotr Il'yich Tchaikovsky
Op. 39

2. Зимнее утро
[Winter Morning]

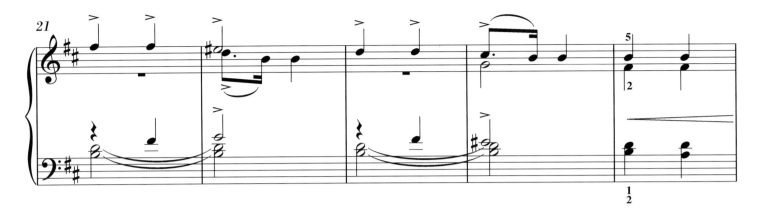

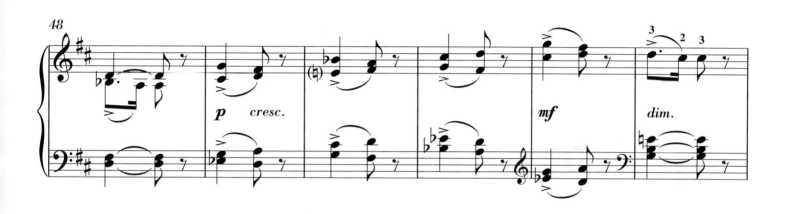

3. Мама
[Mama]

Умеренно [Moderate] (♩ = 88-92)

p с большим чувством и нежностью [*with much feeling and tenderness*]

legatissimo

poco più **f**

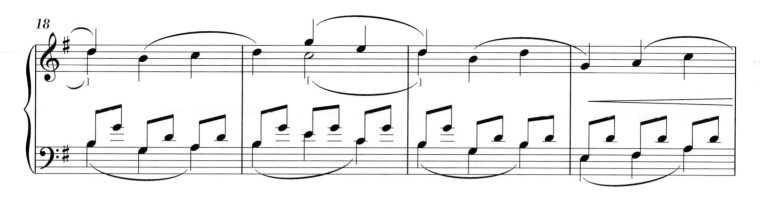

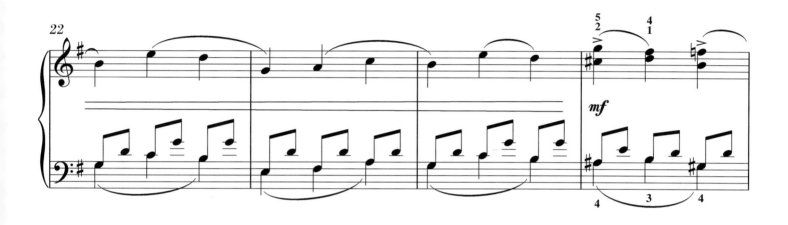

18

4. Игра в лошадки
[Hobbyhorse]

Очень скоро [Very fast] (♩. = 110-120)

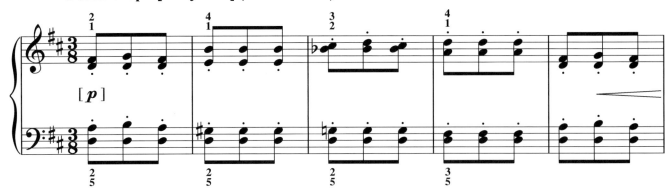

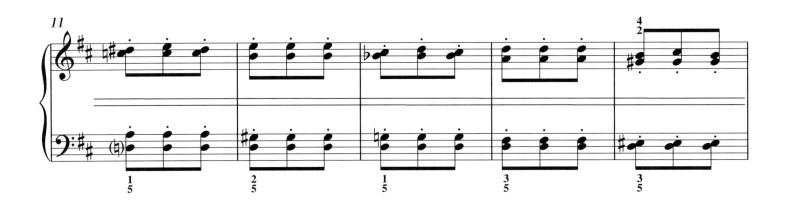

LABORUM
DULCE
LENIMEN

G. SCHIRMER

5. Марш деревянных солдатиков
[The Wooden Soldiers' March]

Умеренно [Moderate] (♩ = 105-115)

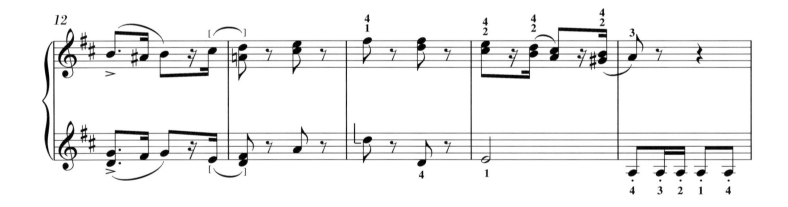

6. Новая кукла
[The New Doll]

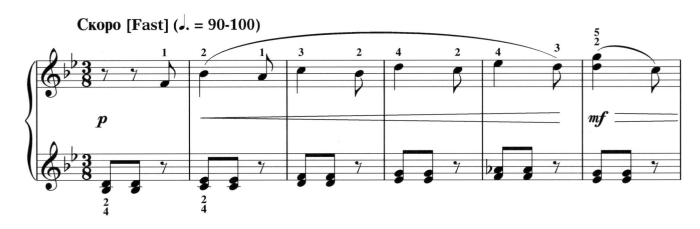

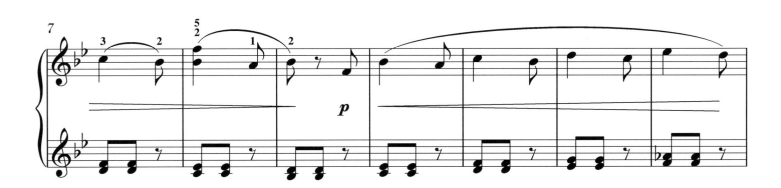

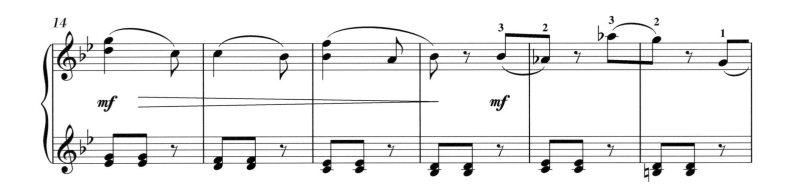

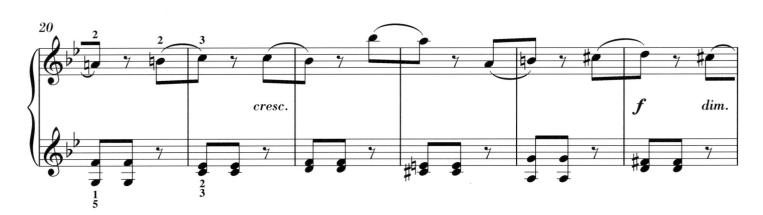

7. Болезнь куклы
[The Doll's Illness]

Умеренно [Moderate] (♩ = 60-64)

8. Похороны куклы
[The Doll's Funeral]

Медленно [Slow] (♩ = 58-62)

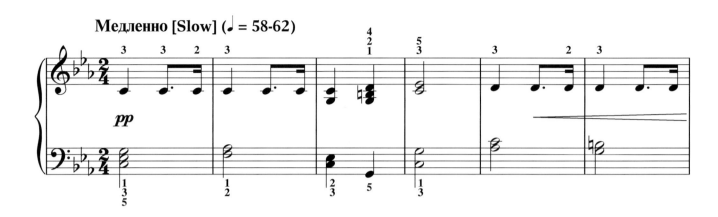

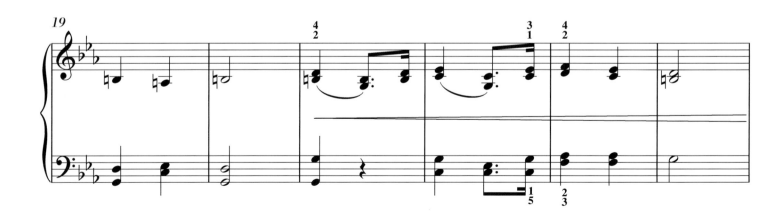

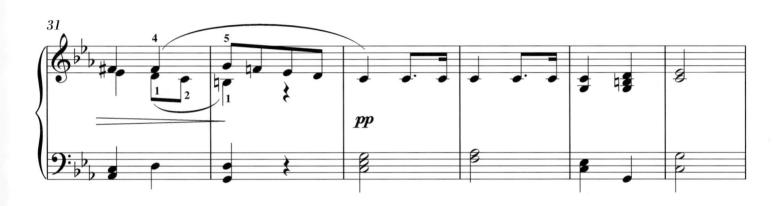

9. Вальс
[Waltz]

Довольно скоро [Quite fast] (♩. = 62-66)

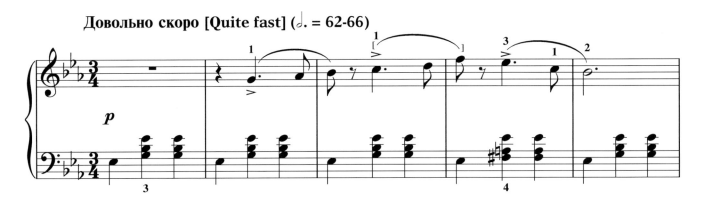

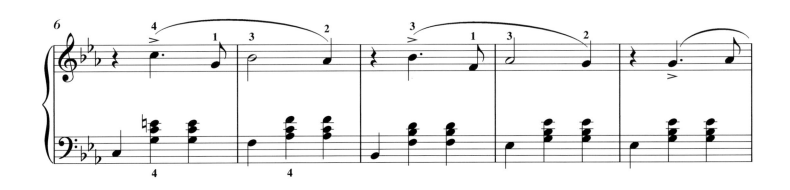

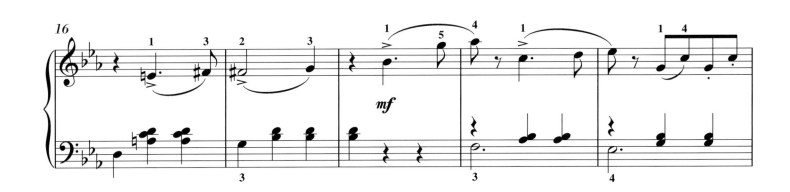

10. Полька
[Polka]

Умеренно (темп польки) [Moderate (Polka tempo)] (♩ = 96-100)

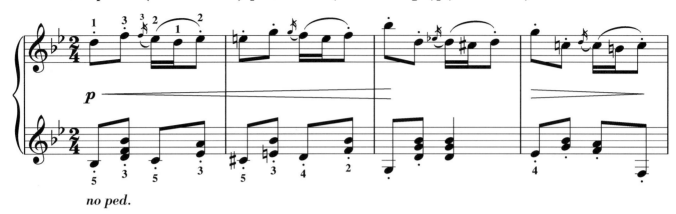

no ped.

11. Мазурка
[Mazurka]

Не очень скоро (темп мазурки) [Not very fast (Mazurka tempo)] (♩. = 45-50)

12. Русская песня
[Russian Song]

Скоро [Fast] (♩ = 100-110)

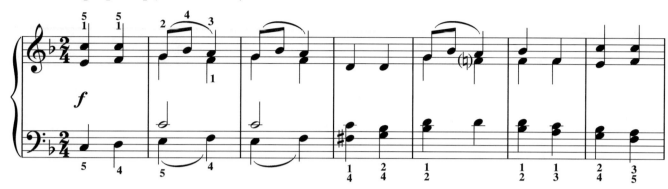

13. Мужик на гармонике играет
[Peasant Plays on the Accordion]

Довольно медленно [Quite slow] ($\quarternote$ = 60-65)

14. Камаринская
[Kamarinskaya]

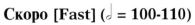

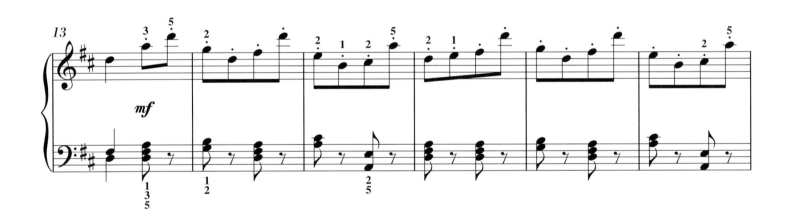

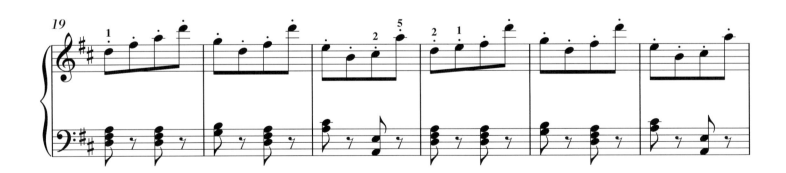

44

15. Итальянская песенка
[Little Italian Song]

Умеренно [Moderate] (♩. = 60-64)

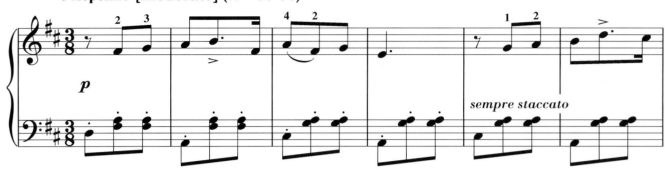

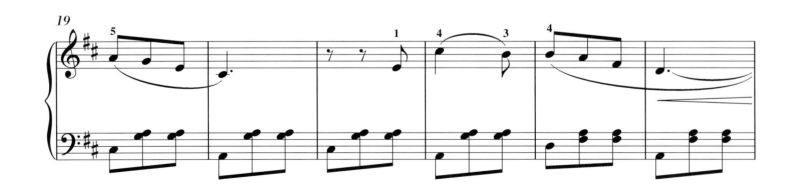

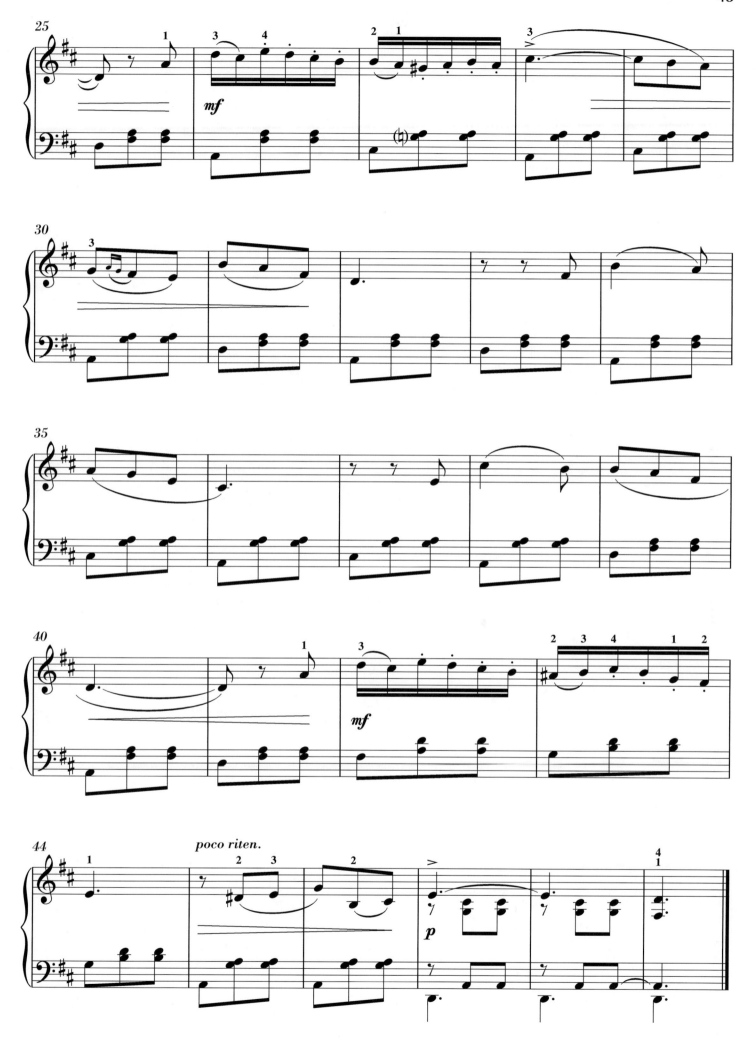

16. Старинная французская песенка
[Little Ancient French Song]

Весьма умеренно [Very moderate] (♩ = 68-72)
с чувством [with feeling]

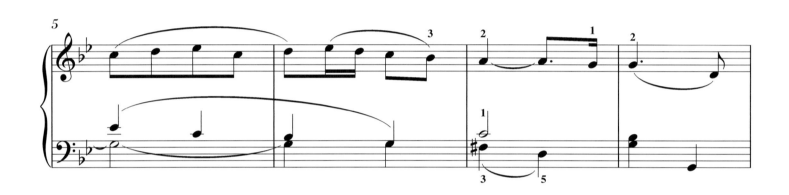

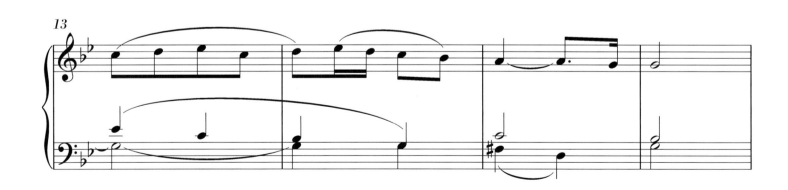

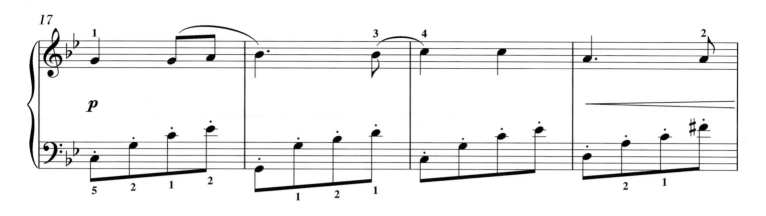

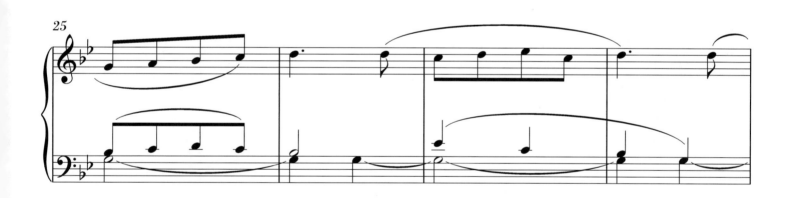

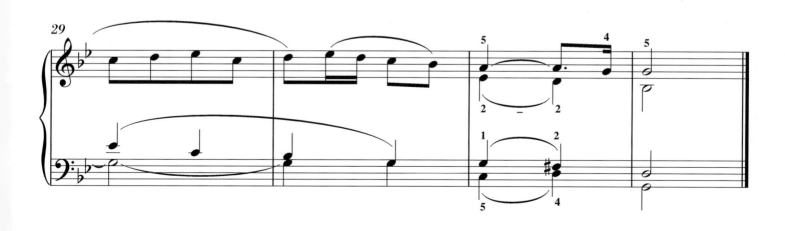

17. Немецкая песенка
[Little German Song]

Очень умеренно [Very moderate] (♩ = 100-110)

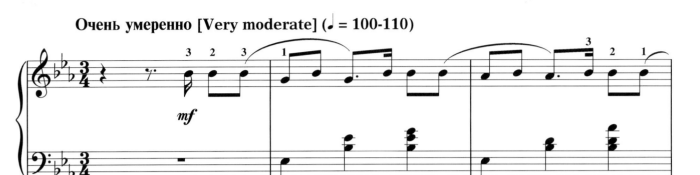

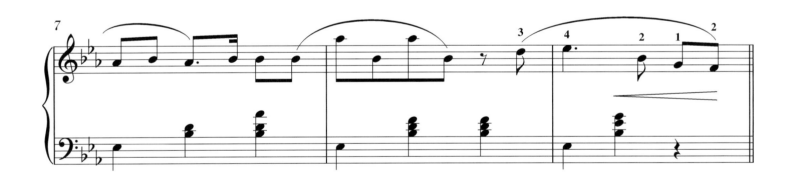

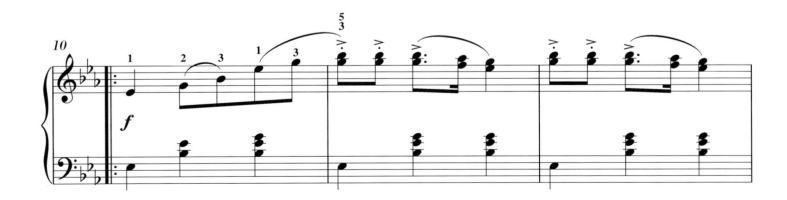

18. Неаполитанская песенка
[Little Neapolitan Song]

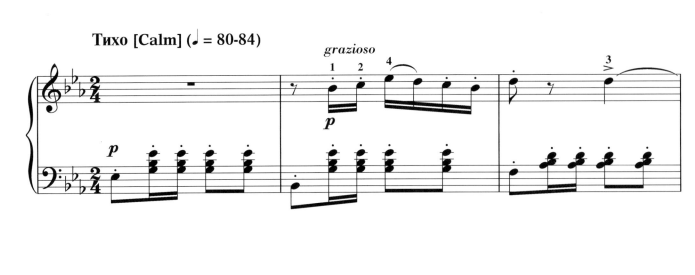

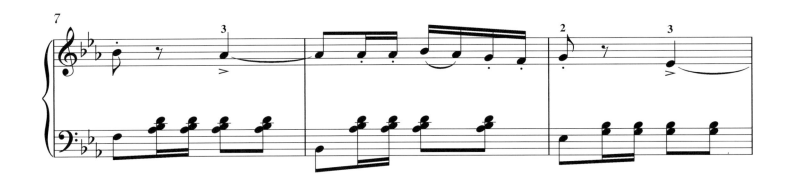

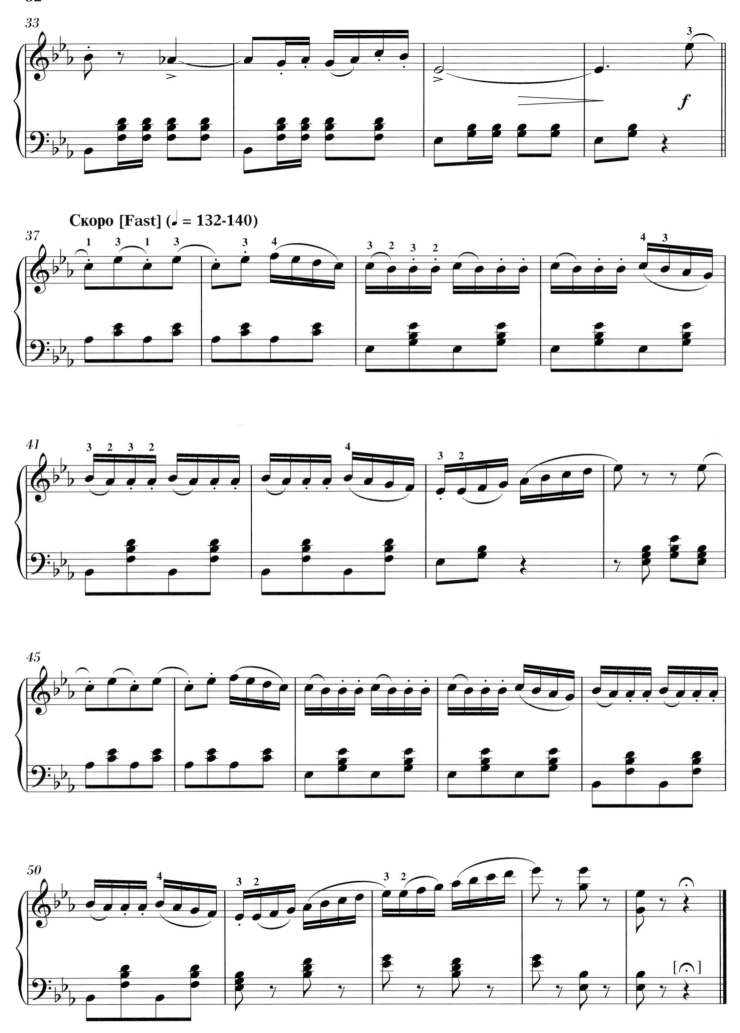

19. Нянина сказка
[Nanny's Tale]

20. Баба-Яга
[Baba-Yaga]

Очень скоро [Very fast] (♩. = 130-140)

21. Сладкая грёза
[Sweet Dream]

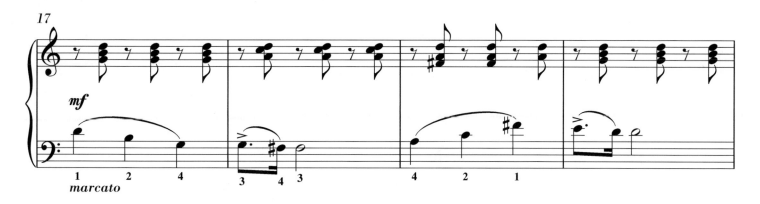

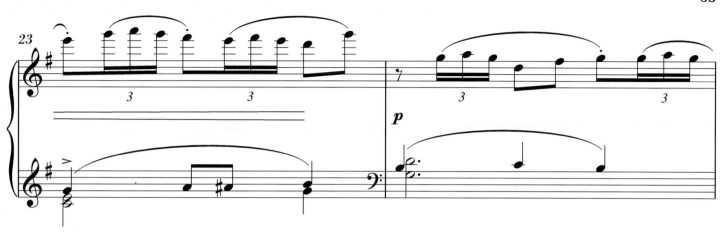

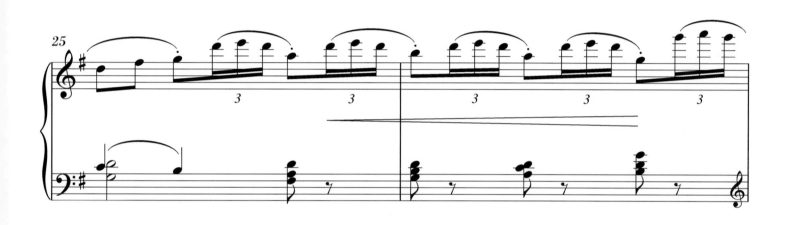

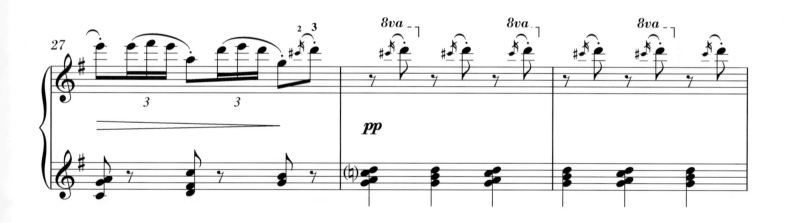

23. В церкви
[At Church]

Умеренно [Moderate] (♩ = 58-62)

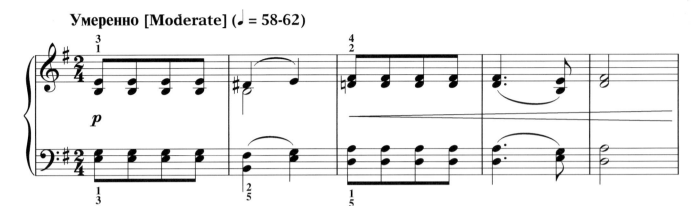

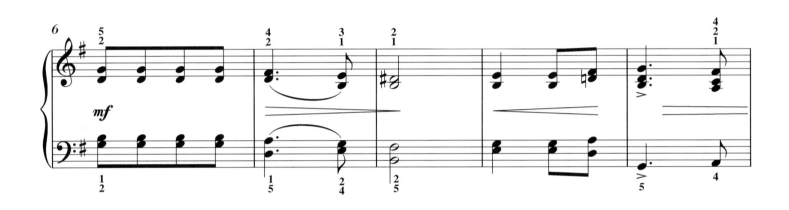

24. Шарманщик поёт
[The Organ-Grinder Sings]

Тихо [Calm] (♩ = 120-130)

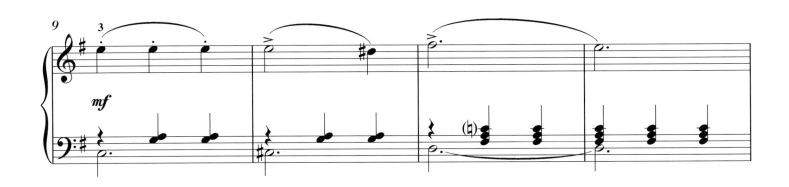

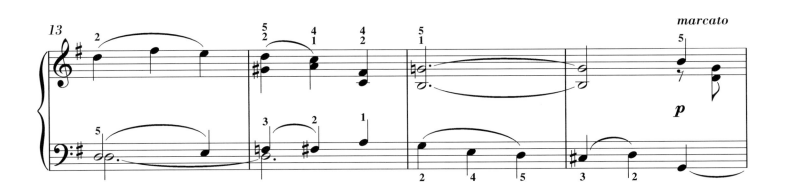

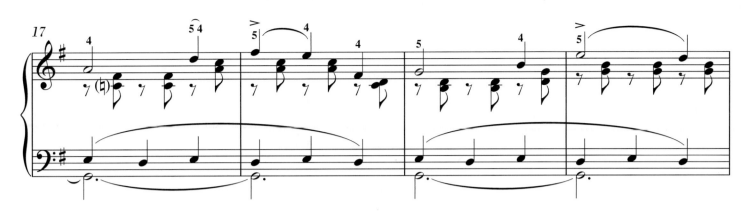

ABOUT THE EDITOR

ALEXANDRE DOSSIN

Considered by Martha Argerich an "extraordinary musician" and by international critics a "phenomenon" and "a master of contrasts," Alexandre Dossin keeps active performing, recording, and teaching careers.

Born in Brazil, where he lived until he was nineteen, Dossin spent nine years studying in Moscow, Russia, before establishing residency in the United States. This background allows him to be fluent in several languages and equally comfortable in a wide range of piano repertoire.

Currently on the faculty of the University of Oregon School of Music, Dossin is a graduate from the University of Texas-Austin and the Moscow Tchaikovsky Conservatory in Russia. He studied with and was an assistant of Sergei Dorensky at the Tchaikovsky Conservatory, and William Race and Gregory Allen at UT-Austin.

A prizewinner in several international piano competitions, Dossin received the First Prize and the Special Prize at the 2003 Martha Argerich International Piano Competition in Buenos Aires, Argentina. Other awards include the Silver Medal and Second Honorable Mention in the Maria Callas Grand Prix and Third Prize and Special Prize in the Mozart International Piano Competition.

He performed numerous live recitals for public radio in Texas, Wisconsin, and Illinois, including returning engagements at the Dame Myra Hess Memorial Concert Series. Dossin has performed in over twenty countries, including international festivals in Japan, Canada, the United States, Brazil, and Argentina, on some occasions sharing the stage with Martha Argerich. He was a soloist with the Brazilian Symphony, Buenos Aires Philharmonic, Mozarteum Symphony, and São Paulo Symphony, having collaborated with renowned conductors such as Charles Dutoit, Michael Gielen, Isaac Karabtchevsky, Keith Clark, and Eleazar de Carvalho.

Dossin has CDs released by Musicians Showcase Recording (2002), Blue Griffin (*A Touch of Brazil*, 2005), and Naxos (*Verdi-Liszt Paraphrases*, 2007; *Kabalevsky Complete Sonatas and Sonatinas*, 2009; *Kabalevsky Complete Preludes*, 2009), praised in reviews by *Diapason*, *The Financial Times*, *Fanfare Magazine*, *American Record Guide*, *Clavier* and other international publications.

In the United States, Alexandre Dossin was featured as the main interview and on the cover of *Clavier* magazine and interviewed by *International Piano Magazine* (South Korea). He is an editor and recording artist for several Schirmer Performance Editions.

Dossin is a member of the Board of Directors for the American Liszt Society and the President of the Oregon Chapter of the American Liszt Society. He lives in the beautiful south hills of Eugene with his wife Maria, and children Sophia and Victor. www.dossin.net